TRADES AND OCCUPATIONS

A Pictorial Archive from Early Sources

Edited by

Carol Belanger Grafton

DOVER PUBLICATIONS, INC., New York

Published in Canada by General Publishing Company, Ltd., 30 Lesmill Road, Don Mills, Toronto, Ontario.
Published in the United Kingdom by Constable and Company, Ltd.

Trades and Occupations: A Pictorial Archive from Early Sources is a new work, first published by Dover Publications, Inc., in 1990.

DOVER *Pictorial Archive* SERIES

Manufactured in the United States of America
Dover Publications, Inc., 31 East 2nd Street, Mineola, N.Y. 11501

Library of Congress Cataloging-in-Publication Data

Trades and occupations : a pictorial archive from early sources / edited by Carol Belanger Grafton.
      p.   cm. — (Dover pictorial archive series)
   ISBN 0-486-26362-2
   1. Occupations in art. 2. Prints—Themes, motives. I. Grafton, Carol Belanger. II. Series.
NE962.025T73   1990
760'.04493059—dc20   90-3298
                                              CIP

CONTENTS

PUBLISHER'S NOTE

This rich volume, with its more than 1100 illustrations spanning some 350 years, constitutes a browser's trove and an unusual resource for designers and artists. The illustrations are of a kind that can hardly be found in any other present-day source, since the periodicals of the last century (the largest source of the images here) have been submerged with the passage of time, along with their extraordinary pictorial wealth.

The depictions remind us that work was for centuries a common subject for art, and particularly for illustration. Pictures of work are perhaps less favored now; the work ethic seems weaker, and the print and electronic media tend to avoid showing workplaces that cannot be made to seem glamorous. The varieties of manufacturing have also become less distinctive and pictorially interesting with the passing years as handwork has waned. (The attributes of the Industrial Revolution, which so transformed the reality of work, can be seen here side by side with those of the pre-industrial era.)

Substantial verisimilitude can be sensed in most of these images, which only infrequently appear to be idealized to the point of distortion. Despite some use of attractive models and some aesthetically dictated composition, the hard actuality of many occupations is rarely disguised by smiling faces or graceful attitudes.

The sources that Carol Belanger Grafton has mined for this collection are numerous and varied. *The Illustrated London News, Chatterbox, The Graphic,* and especially *Punch* account for many of the English pictures. *Scientific American, Harper's Weekly, Harper's Monthly, The Youth's Companion, Frank Leslie's Illustrated Newspaper,* and the anonymous 1807 *Book of Trades, or Library of the Useful Arts* supplied most of the American images. The French *La Nature* provided many depictions, as did the German *Fliegende Blätter, Ueber Land und Meer,* and the 1568 *Ständebuch* (Book of Trades) illustrated by Jost Amman. The whimsicality of the cartoons and story illustrations contrasts with the didacticism of the trade books and the undecorative and straightforward style of the serious journals.

This wide-ranging anthology of engravings, woodcuts, and drawings should fill an important niche in many private iconographic libraries.

Note: A few of the illustrations may appear in seemingly anomalous categories; see the Index for the most detailed and accurate trade designations.

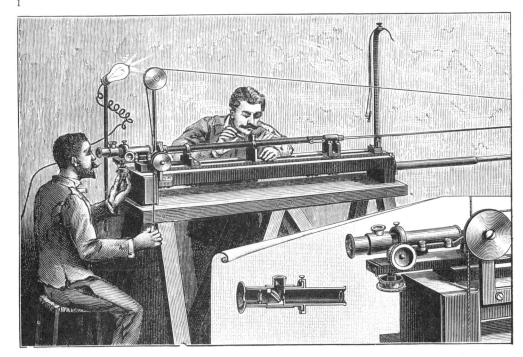

2   Armament Workers

4   Art and Antique Dealers

16

17

18

19

The SCULPTOR

The ARCHITECT

26

27

28

29

30

31

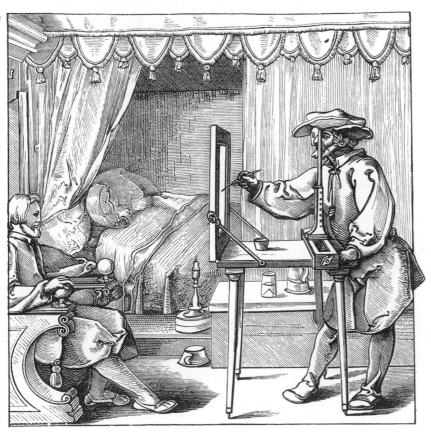

2 million

10,000 years Ago
Neolythic
- 8000 - 3000 BC
farm
oldest
3000 BC Temple Builders

250,000 - AXE found
5,000 year ago.
3100, BC writting
6000 - TRading
YEAR Ago
7000 BC settled Down

MUST BE SOLD

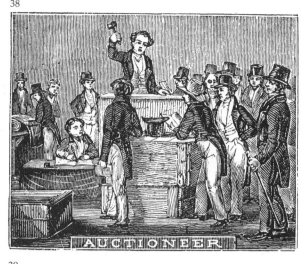

AUCTIONEER

VENDUE this Day

AUCTION SALE LIVE STOCK &c

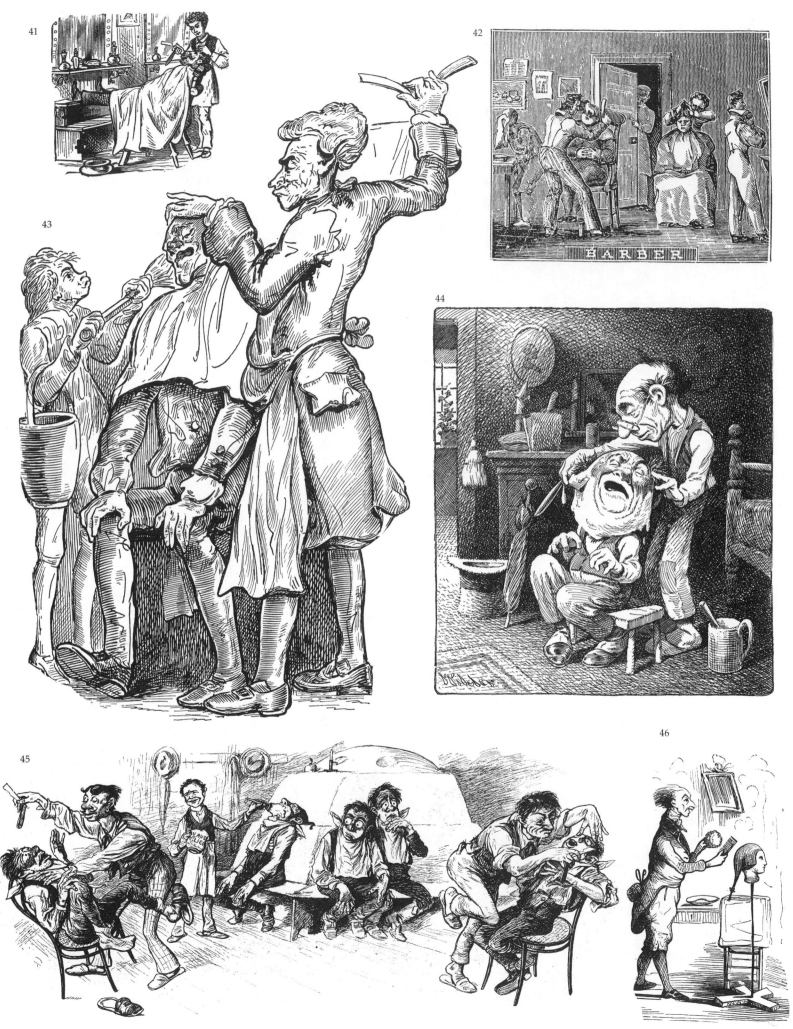

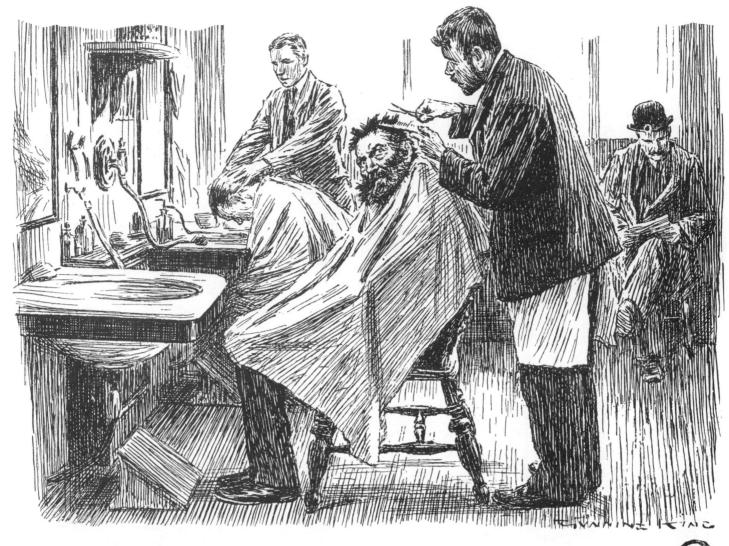

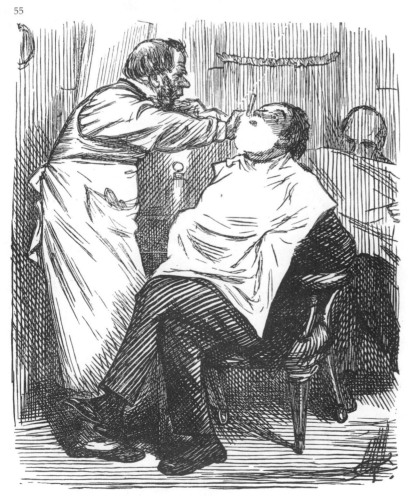

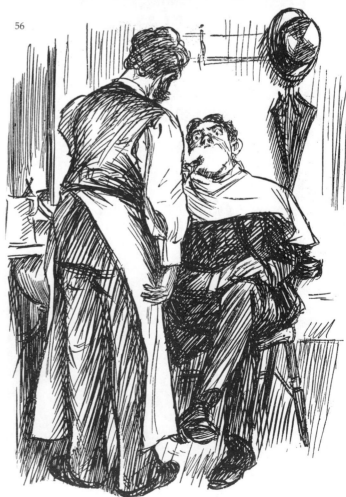

57

58

59

60

61

Barrel and Crate Makers 15

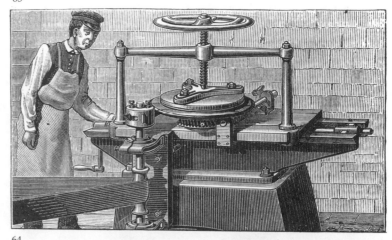

16   Barrel and Crate Makers

66

67

68

69

70

71

18   Basketmakers

BLACKSMITH

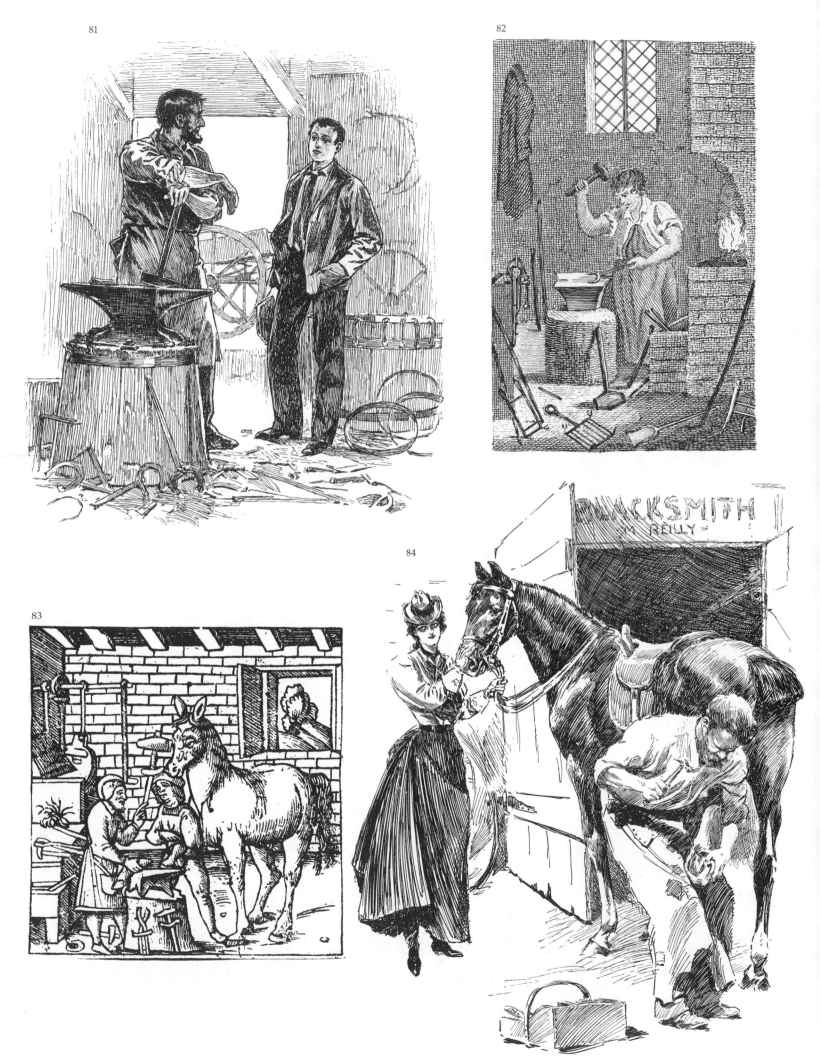

81

82

84

83

85

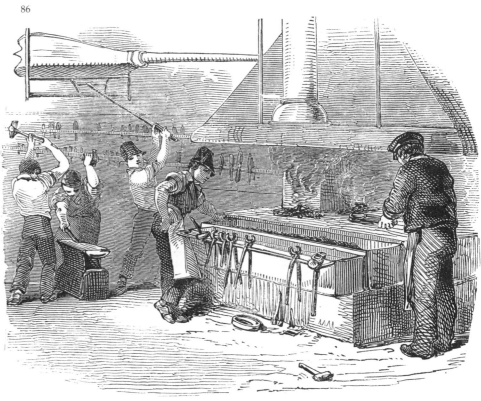

86

87

88

89

90

94

95

96

97

98

99

100

101

Brewers, Winemakers, and Distillers   25

103

104

105

106

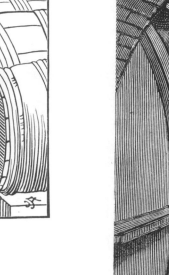

107

108

109

110

111

112

113

114

115

116

117

118

28   Brewers, Winemakers, and Distillers

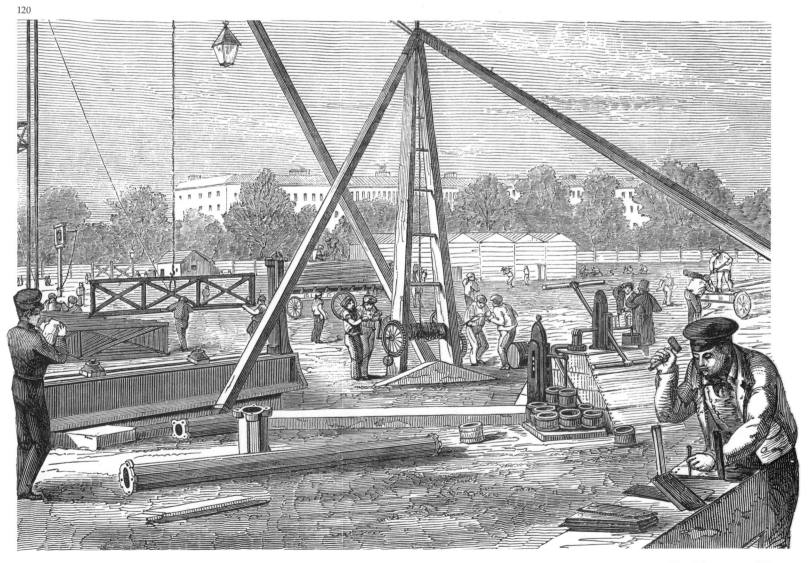

128

129

130

131

132

133

134

135

34   Candlemakers

142

143

144

145

146

147

148

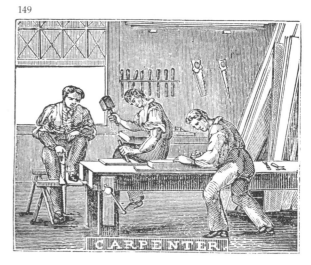
149

150

151

152

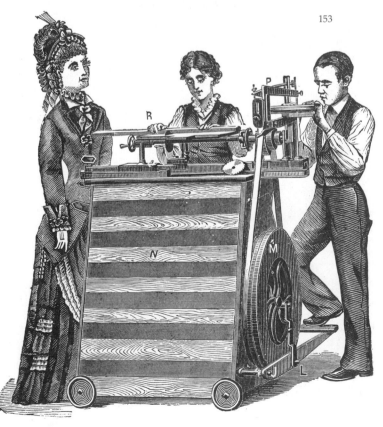

153

154

155

156

157

158

159

160

162

161

Carpenters   37

168

169

170

171

172

173

Carters, Cabbies, and Coachmen 39

174

175

176

177

178

179

180

181

The CLERGYMAN

Clerks and Officeworkers   47

225

226

227

228

229

230

231

232

233

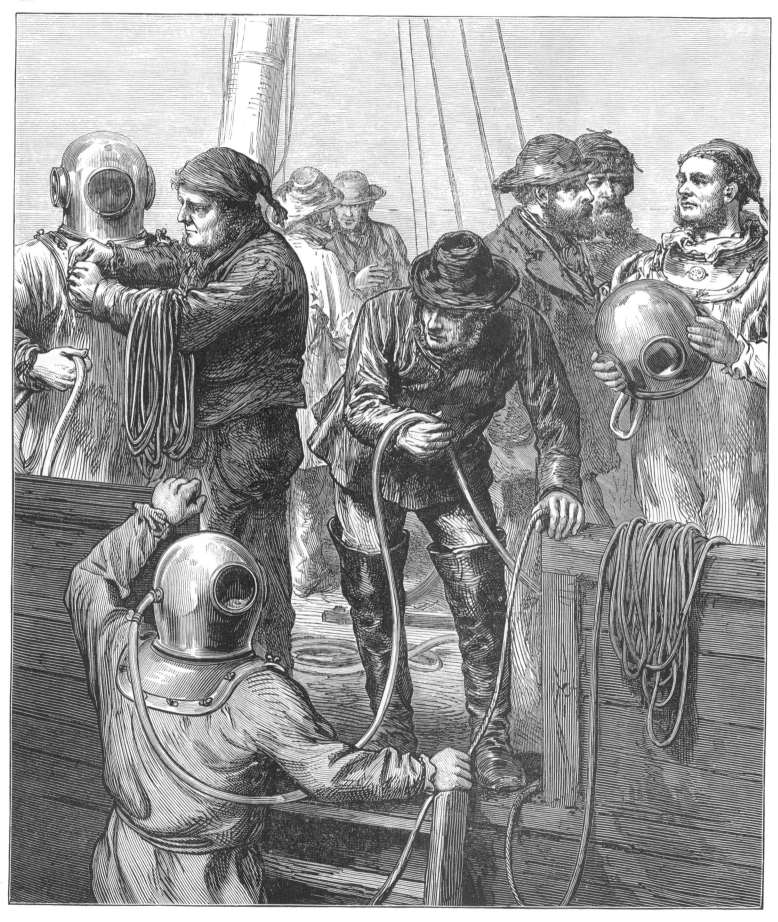

241

242

243

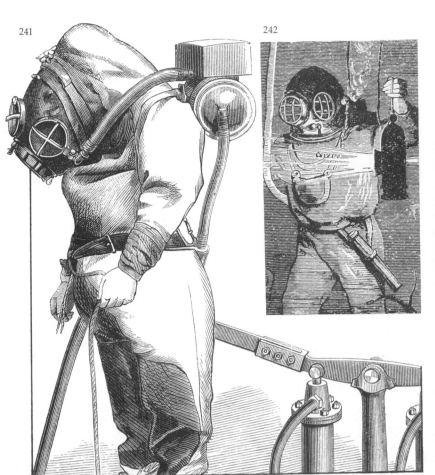

244

245

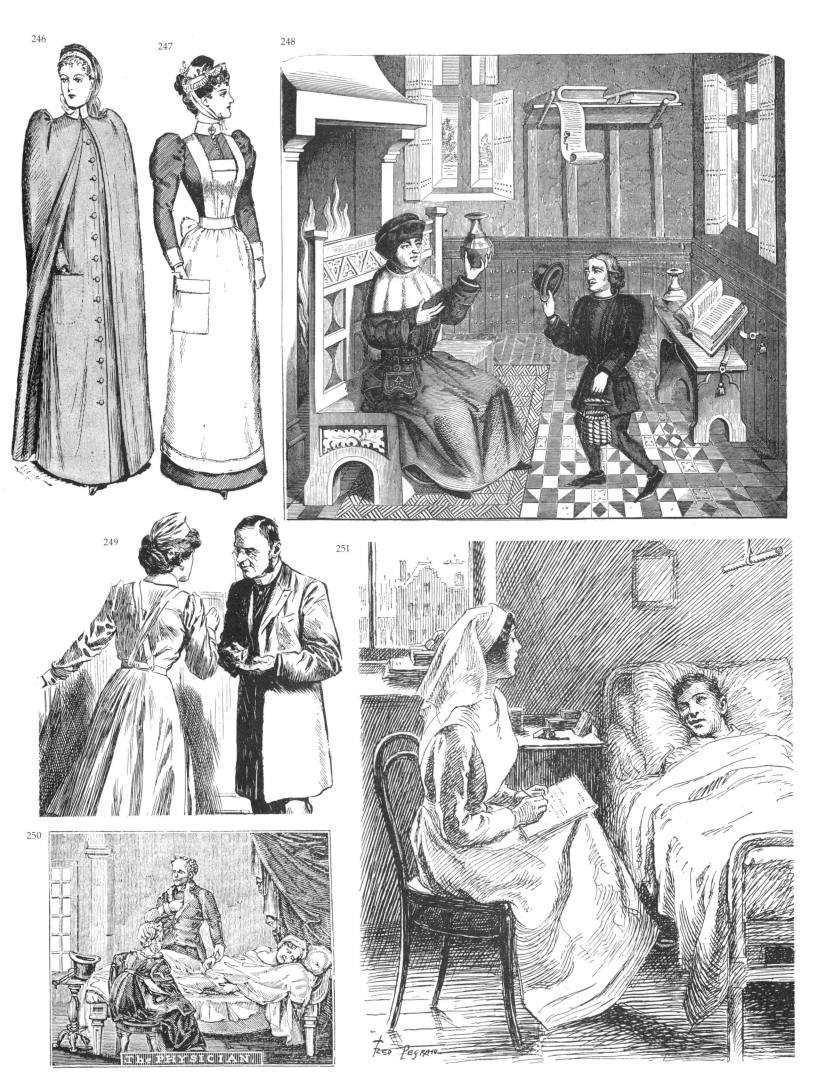

246 247 248

249 251

250 The PHYSICIAN

252

253

254

255

256

257

-A.T.SMITH-

259

260

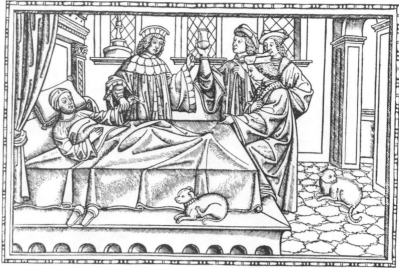

261

262

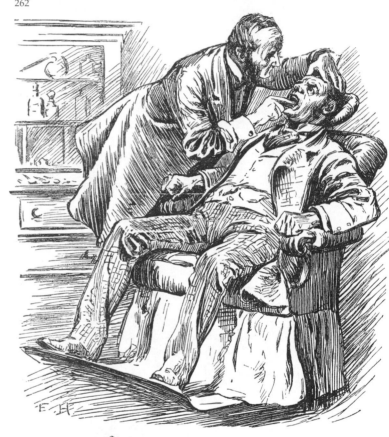

263

264

275 276 277 278

279 280 281 282

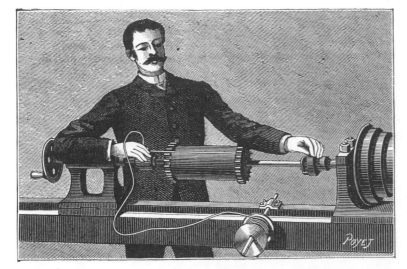

290

291

292

293

294

295

296

297

298

303

304

305

306

307

308

309

310

311

312

313

314

315

316

317

318

319

320

321

FARMER

322

323

324

325

326

335

336

337

338

339

340

341

342

343

344

345

346

347

348

349

IN BOND

PAYING TELLER   RECEIVING TELLER   CASHIER

NEW PRIMROSE

Financiers, Bankers, and Stockbrokers 71

358

359

360

361

362

363

364

366

367

368

369

WHALER

370

371

372

373

374

375

76   Fishermen

377

378

379

380

381

382

383

384

78   Flower Sellers and Nurseryworkers

Flower Sellers and Nurseryworkers　79

387

388

389

390

392

391

393

394

80   Food Preparers, Sellers, and Servers

395

396

397

398

401

402

403

404

405

406

407

408

409 410 411 412

413

415

414

Food Preparers, Sellers, and Servers 83

Food Preparers, Sellers, and Servers

423

424

425

426

427

428

429

430

431

432

433

434

435

436

437

438

439

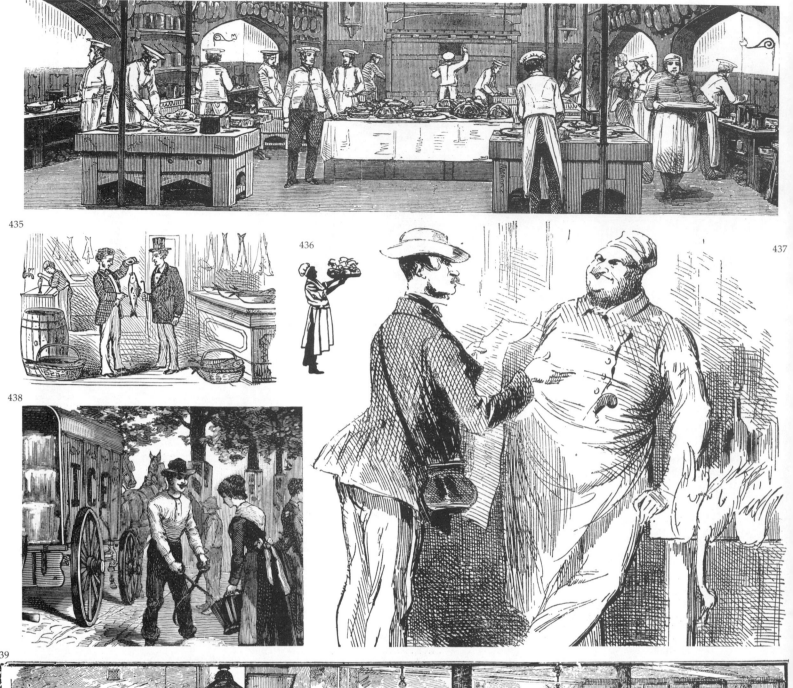

440

441

442

443

444

445

446

447

448

449

450

451

452

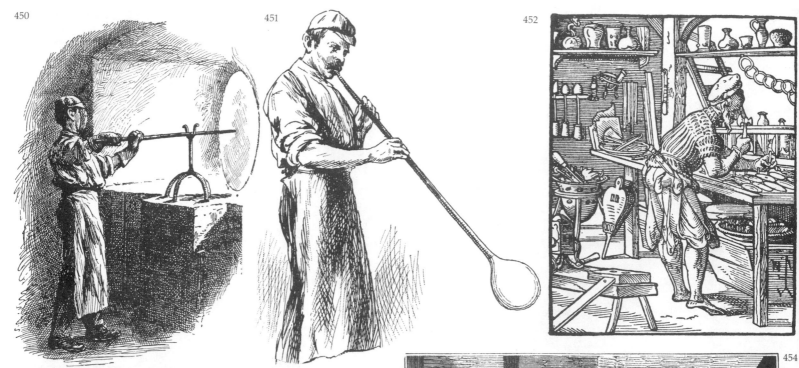

453

454

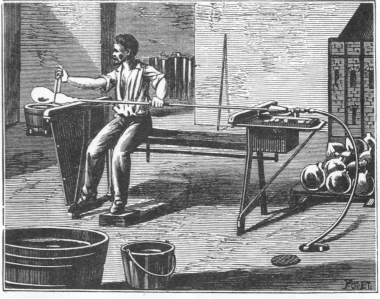

455

456

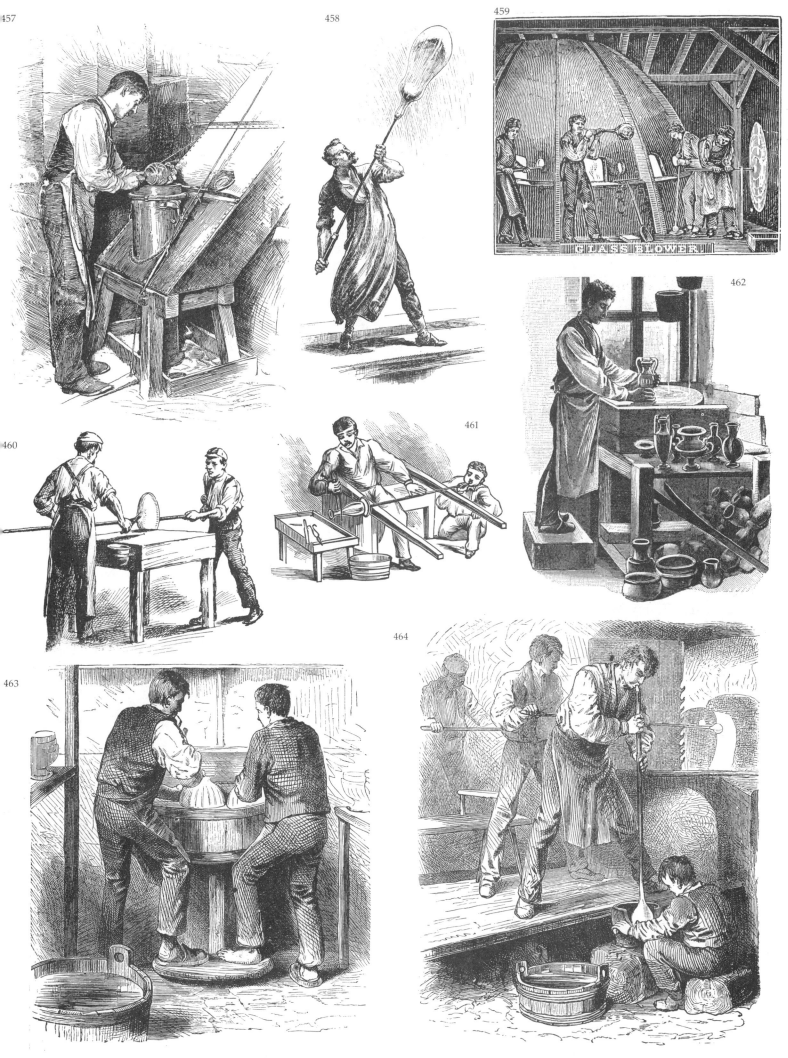

GLASS BLOWER!

465

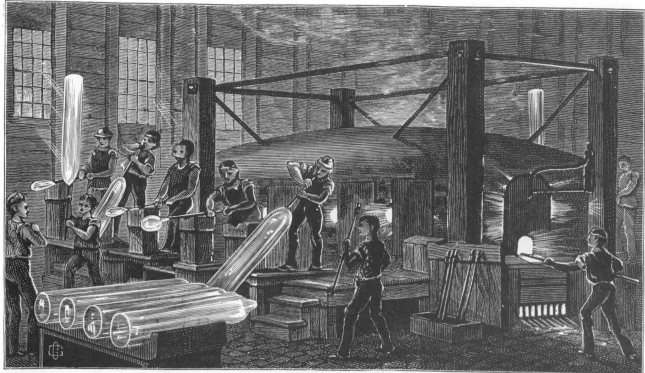

466

467

468

90   Glass Workers

470

471

472

473

476

477

478

479

482

483

484

485

486

487

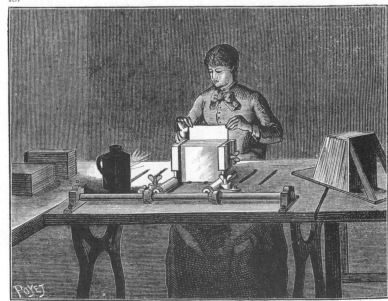

488

489

490

491

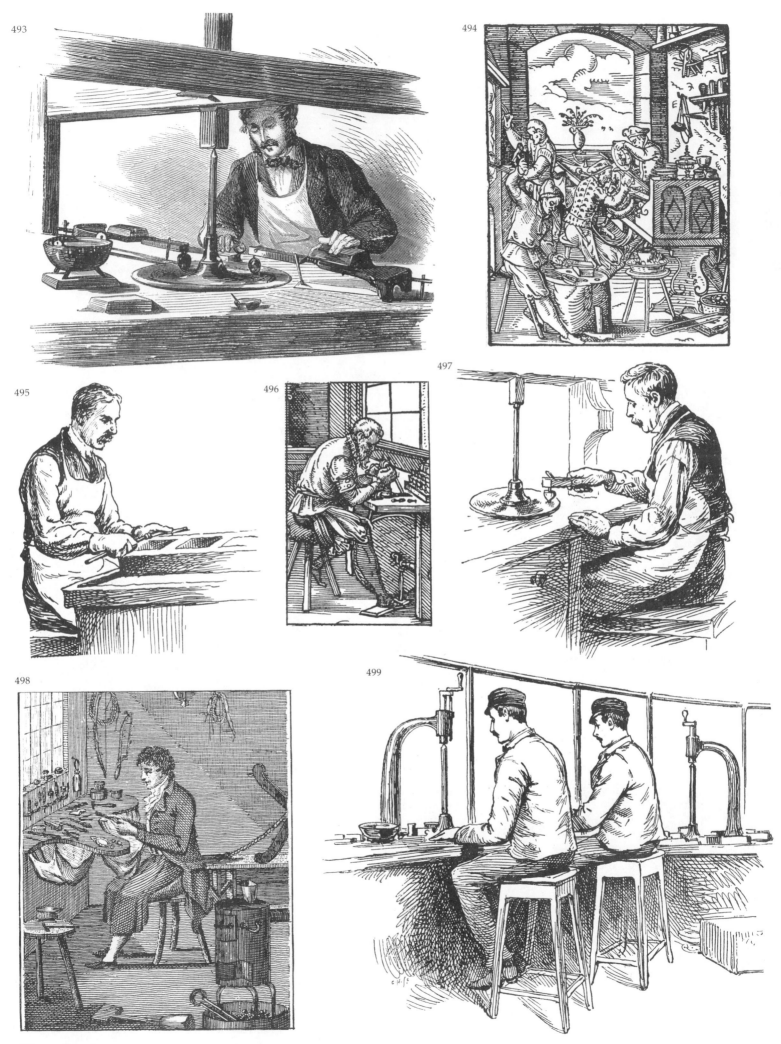

502

503

504

506

505

507

509

510

511

512

513

514

515

516

517

518

519

520

521

522

523

524

525

526

527

528

529

530

531

532

533

534

535

536

537

538

539

540

541

Laundry Workers

544

546

547

548

549

550

The LAWYER

551

110   Lawyers and Judges

552

553

554

555

556

557

558

559

561

560

562

A   B

563

564

565

566

567

568

569

570

571

572

573

574

575

576

577

578

579

580

581

582

583

584

585

586

587

118 Metalworkers and Foundrymen

601

602

603

604

605

606

120　　Metalworkers and Foundrymen

615

616

617

618

619

620

621

622

623

624

625

626

627

628

629

630

631

632

Newspaper Workers and Sellers   127

643

644

645

646

647

648

649

657

658

659

660

661

662

663   664   665

666

675   676   677

678

679

680   681

I WAS BORN CRIPPLE

HO + BUNS

Peddlers and Vendors   133

696

697

SOUHAITS de BONHEUR et de SANTÉ A NOS LECTEURS 1897

ADIEU 1896!!!!!

698

699

700

701

702

703
704
705
707
708
706
709
710
711

Programme 15 centimes

727 728 729 730 731 732 733 734 735

736

737

738

739

740

741

742

743

744

745

746

747

748

749

750

751

752

753

754

755

756

757

771   772   773

774   775

776

785 786 787

788 789

790 791 792

793

818

819

820

821

822

823

824

825

826

Potters and Ceramic Workers   151

832

833

834

835

836

837

838

839

840

841

842

843

844

845

846

847

848

849

850

851

852

853

854

855

856

857

858

859

860

861

862

863

871

872

873

874

875

876

877

878

879

880

881

882

883

884

885

886

887

888

889

Scientists and Alchemists

894

895

896

897

898

164   Scientists and Alchemists

899

900

901

902

903

904

905

906

907

908

SHIPWRIGHT

909

10

911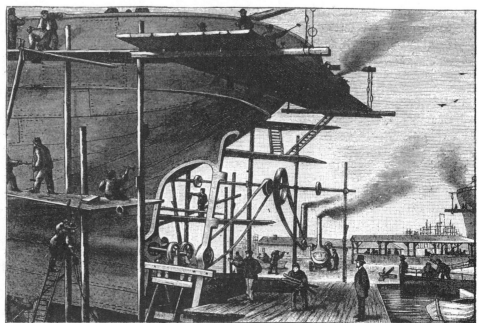

912

913

914

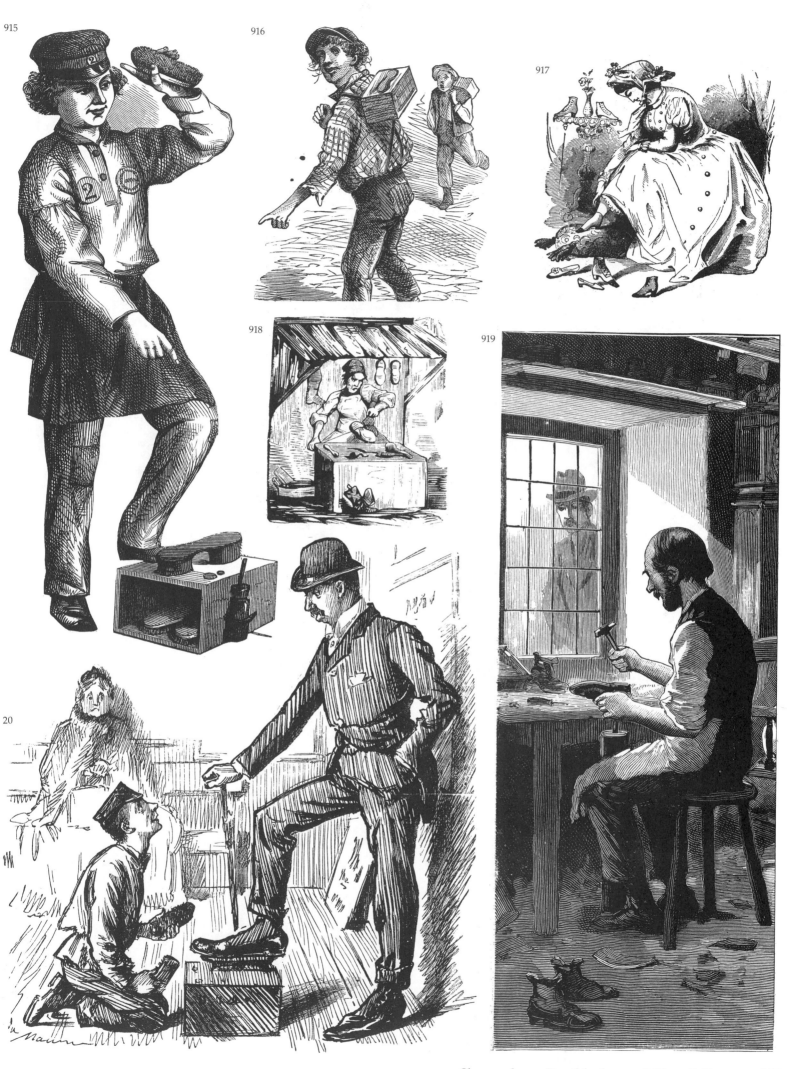

915

916

917

918

919

20

Shoemakers, Bootblacks, and Shoe Sellers

928

929

930

MERCHANT

931

Shopkeepers and Merchants 171

932 933 934 935 937 936

938

939

940

941

942

943

944

945

946

948

947

949

950

951

952

953

954

975

976

977

978

979

980

981

982

983

984

996

997

999

998

1000

1001

1002

1019

1020

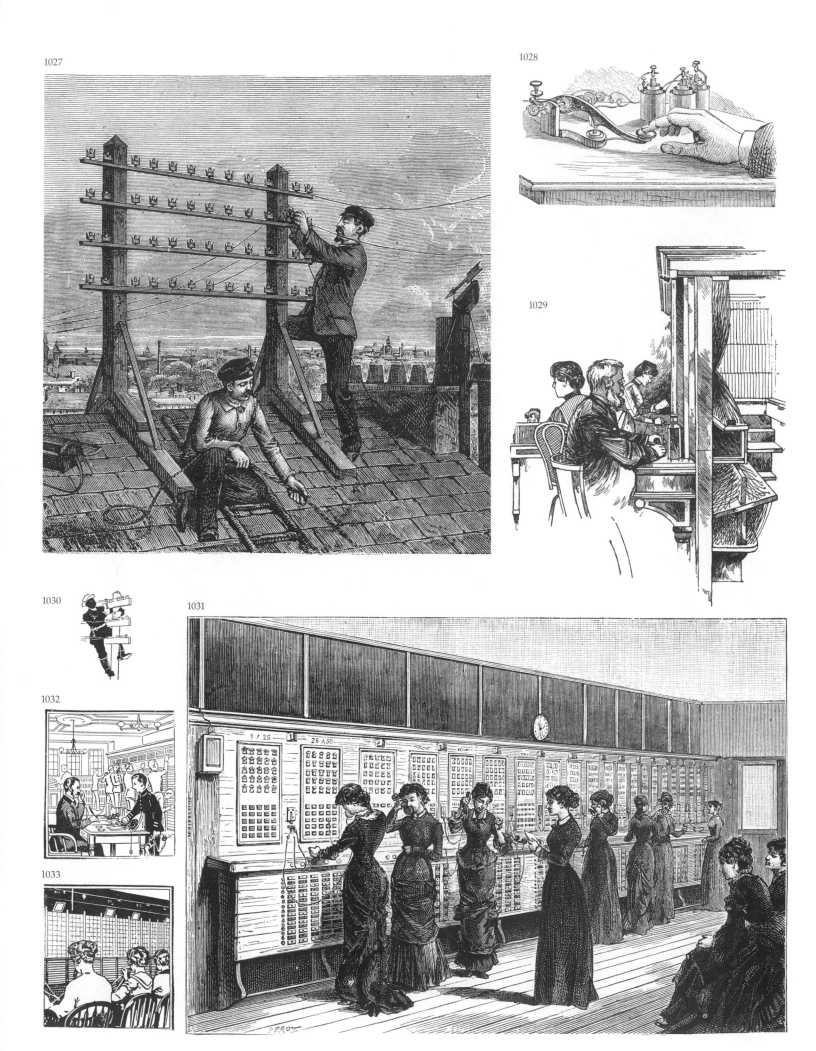

186   Telephone and Telegraph Workers

1042

1043

1044

1045

K

1046

DRESSMAKING DEPARTMENT

1047

1048

1049

1050

1051

1052

1053

1054

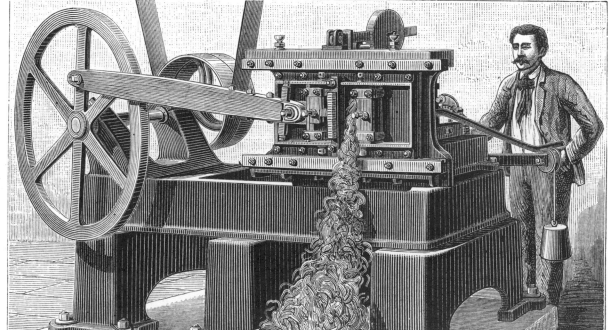

1055

1056

1057

1058

1059

1060

1061

1062

1063

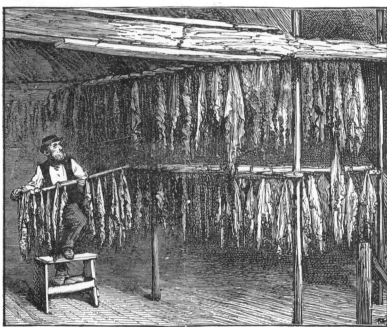

1065

1064

1066

1067

194   Tobacco Workers and Merchants

1069

1070

1071

1072

1073

1074

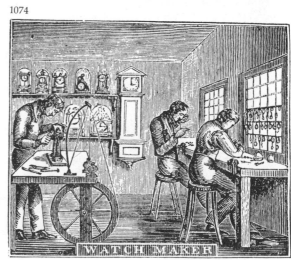

1075

1076

1077

1078

1079

1080

1081

1082

1083

1084

1085

1086

1087

1089

1088

1090

1094

1095

1096

1097

1098

1099

1100

INDEX TO
ILLUSTRATIONS

The numbers are those of the illustrations, not the pages.